National Museums Scotland

Supernatural Scotland

Eileen Dunlop
with illustrations by Sheila Cant

SCOTTIES SERIES EDITORS
Frances and Gordon Jarvie

Contents

Published in 2011 by
NMS Enterprises Limited – Publishing
a division of NMS Enterprises Limited
National Museums Scotland
Chambers Street, Edinburgh EH1 1JF

Text © Eileen Dunlop 2011

Images (for © information see below and page
viii of the Facts and activities section)

ISBN: 978-1-905267-36-1

British Library Cataloguing in Publication Data
A catalogue record of this book
is available from the British Library.

Book design concept by Redpath.
Cover design by Mark Blackadder.
Layout by NMSE – Publishing.
Printed and bound in the United Kingdom by
Bell & Bain Ltd, Glasgow.

CREDITS

*Thanks are due to the following individuals and
organisations who supplied images and photographs for this publication. Every attempt has
been made to contact copyright holders to use the
material in this publication. If any image has been
inadvertently missed, please contact the publisher.*

*The author wishes to thank Ron Chisholm, one of
the architects who restored Haddington House,
for the story of the ghostly horse (see p. 4). Thanks
are also due to Neil G. W. Curtis, Senior Curator,
Marischal Museum, Aberdeen, for information
about the Inuit kayaker (see p. 17).*

COVER ILLUSTRATIONS (© National Museums
Scotland) for the watchtower, Edinburgh and the
miniature coffins found on Arthur's Seat, Edinburgh.

NATIONAL MUSEUMS SCOTLAND
(© National Museums Scotland) for pp 2 (Mexican
boat and watchtower); 3 (gravestone and etching
of Culloden 1797 by Laurie and Whittle); 4 (horse
by William Shiels 1785-1857); 5 (Ann Street and
Glamis Castle); 6 (James VI/I, joug); 7 (witches); 8
(guisers); 10 (elf bolt); 13 (hay-mowing); 14 (water);
15 ('A Fish out of Water' soft sculpture by Susan
Brotchie 1985, and vase depicting mermaid by
Gerda Stromberg 1936); 17 (Inuit kayak model);
20 ('Nessie' postcard); 21 (snuffbox); 22 (adder-
stones and Callanish); 25 (Clootie Well); 26 (Pictish
stone); 27 (dog by William Shiels); 29 (Flannan
Isle); 32 (St Andrew and Whithorn hoard); 35
(sheep by William Shiels); 36 (Charles II locket);
39 (Robert the Bruce statue); Facts and activities
section, page i (Tam o' Shanter engraving)

FURTHER CREDITS (p. viii of Facts and acti
section)

SCOTTIE BOOKS

For a full listing of NMS Enterprises Lin
Publishing titles and related merchand
www.nms.ac.uk/books

Ghosts and graveyards

Since the beginning of time, people have believed that spirits of the dead haunt places where they lived. Every country in the world has its own ghost stories.

Mexican 'Days of the Dead' boat complete with Death in the front and some Mexican musicians!

In Scotland, the belief flourished in the ill-lit streets of the towns and cities, and the lonely glens and hills, where it was easy to imagine on a dark winter night that a ghost might be flitting behind you. Ghosts did not appear simply to frighten people – sometimes they came to right a wrong done in life, like stealing money or cheating a relative out of a title or property. Sometimes they were murderers who had been denied Christian burial and could not rest in their lonely graves.

A watchful eye!

The watchtower in St Cuthbert's kirkyard in Edinburgh's West End was built in the early 1800s to protect newly-buried bodies from the bodysnatchers. The Edinburgh Medical College received fewer than five corpses a year for anatomy demonstrations, prompting criminals to dig up fresh bodies from the city's graveyards to sell to anatomists. The notorious William Burke and William Hare, too lazy and impatient to wait, murdered tenants in Hare's boarding house and strangers on the busy streets of Edinburgh. Years later, in 1836, miniature coffins were found on Arthur's Seat in Edinburgh. Their origin is mysterious, but some say that they represent the tragic victims of Burke and Hare.

Naturally ghosts were associated with grave-yards, and memorial stones were carved with skulls and other symbols of death. It was long believed that although spirits were allowed to haunt by night, they must return to their coffins when the cock crowed at dawn.

The second sight

In the Highlands and Islands, a person with 'the second sight', called a **seer**, can foretell events. (The seventh son of a seventh son, and children born on 31 October, Halloween, were believed to have second sight.) The sighting of a ghost often comes before a death. A seer in the island of Coll had a son working away from home. When the seer was digging on his croft, he noticed his son helping him several times. Twice, when he was coming home with a basket of peats and sat down by the road to rest, he saw the boy helping him to lift the basket onto his back. Not long after, news came of his son's death far away.

A Perthshire epitaph

Here lys
James Stewart
He sall rys

The weeping tombstone

In the churchyard of Inchnadamph in Sutherland is a vault, unused since the early 20th century, which holds the bodies of the MacLeod chiefs of Assynt. On one of the flat tombstones there is a spot of damp about ten centimetres across, which never dries out – even in spells of hot weather. The roof is in good repair, the ground is not waterlogged, and no other stone shows any sign of damp. Local tradition claims that before a major catastrophe, such as a war, the moisture turns to blood.

The undead sailor

Three hundred years ago, a Polish ship was wrecked at Sandalwood Bay in Sutherland. Many sailors drowned. It is said that the ghost of one of them often knocks at the door of a certain cottage. Anyone foolish enough to open the door sees a horrifying sight – a headless man outlined against the grey, stormy sea.

Ghost of Culloden

Culloden Moor, Scotland's saddest battle-field, is haunted by a tall Highlander with a pale, tired face. He whispers 'defeated' to all those he meets.

Background: Scene from the Battle of Culloden, 1746.

Haunted houses

For a very small country, Scotland has a very large number of haunted houses!

Large, small, ancient or modern, all have at least one resident ghost. Sometimes the ghost is peaceful, and many people seem to live happily in a haunted house. However, just as often, a malicious ghost causes accidents or destroys people's belongings. The worst are **poltergeists**, invisible beings who make frightening noises and throw objects around. If a ghost is too troublesome, it may be **exorcised** – also called 'laying the ghost'. Exorcism is performed by a priest who prays and orders the ghost to depart.

Some apparitions are more animal than human. The Laird of Haddington had a son who went to fight in the Battle of Flodden in 1513. Although he survived the fighting, on his return the young man was thrown from his horse and fatally injured. The horse galloped home, followed by a groom who broke the tragic news.

Distraught, the laird ran to the stable and pole-axed the horse, cursing the animal for doing to his son what the mighty English army had failed to do.

For many years, rumours persisted of an apparition, a horse's head, which appeared, always in September, in the servants' hall of Haddington House. It was so terrifying that one September during the 1890s the servants shunned the hall. Eighty years later, architects restoring Haddington House discovered an ancient horse's skull under the floor of the servants' quarters. It is intriguing that the Battle of Flodden was fought in September 1513.

Other spooky places ...

Glamis Castle, near Kirriemuir, is Scotland's most haunted castle. Among its ghosts is a terrible monster kept in a secret room. A white lady flits through the garden, a tongueless woman peers through a barred window, while in a stone chair sits a little boy, the ghost of a West Indian servant who was treated unkindly at Glamis.

A mile from Lasswade in Midlothian stands a cottage (above) where the English writer Thomas de Quincey (1785-1829) once lived. His ghost has often been seen wandering along the banks of the river Esk, usually after midnight, swinging the lantern he carried on nocturnal walks.

No 12 Ann Street, Edinburgh (above) was haunted by Mr Swan, who had been sent to sea as a boy and died of homesickness far away. Coming back as a ghost to his childhood home, he was last seen in the 1930s, when the children of the house told their parents of 'the little man in black who comes to say goodnight'.

Thomas de Quincey

GLAMIS CASTLE

The castle was home to the late Queen Mother, Elizabeth Bowes-Lyon. The lands of Glamis were originally given to the Lyon family, possibly by King Robert II of Scotland.

Witches

Today witches are associated with stories and with fun at Halloween, but in the past people took witchcraft far more seriously.

How could you tell a witch? By a birthmark or scar (seen as 'the Devil's mark'), a squint ('the evil eye'), or epilepsy (Devil possession). Common accusations included making people or animals ill, spoiling crops and causing hailstorms. Over 3000 Scots, mostly women, were accused of witchcraft. Around 2000 were executed, usually by strangling and burning.

Although many confessed under torture, enough confessed voluntarily to suggest that they believed in their own powers. Only in the 18th century, when the Church became

King James VI (1566-1625) succeeded his mother, Mary, Queen of Scots, in 1567 and became the first king of Scotland and England in 1603. Superstitious but learned, he ordered the translation of the Bible known as the Authorised or King James Version (1611).

less influential, did the burnings stop and belief in witchcraft wane.

The North Berwick witches

King James VI of Scotland feared witchcraft. On Halloween 1590, two hundred witches were accused of meeting by the seashore at North Berwick with the intention of sinking the ship carrying James and his bride home

A spell for raising a storm

I knot this ragg upon this stane,
To raise the wind in the Devillis name;
It sall not lye til I please again.

A spell against the evil eye

Shake from thee thy harm,
Shake from thee thy jealousy,
Shake from thee thy illness,
In name of Father, Son and
Holy Spirit.

This iron collar or **joug** was used to restrain suspected witches. It comes from Fife and is dated to the 17th century.

Morag of Scourie

At Scourie in Sutherland lived a woman known as Morag the Storm Witch, who sold good winds to sailors for sixpence. She also had spells to change the direction of snowstorms and calm the sea, known locally as 'whistling to the wind'.

from Denmark. James demanded reprisals. One suspect broke down and named others. They were arrested, tortured and tried in Edinburgh before the King.

The witches' confessions were sensational. They admitted sailing in sieves, trying to poison the King with toad's venom, and dancing with the Devil disguised as a dog. Strangely, no one found these claims far-fetched. The witches were executed on Edinburgh's Castle Hill.

White witches

'White witches' used kindly magic to heal people and animals, often by combining herbal drinks and spells. Sometimes they dipped magic stones in water for the patient to drink. But if the cure failed or the patient died, their 'white magic' might be denounced as black.

How to destroy the enemy

A witch who wanted to kill someone first made a figure out of clay. She pierced it with pins and placed it in a stream. Supposedly, as it disintegrated in the water, the person cursed similarly wasted away.

The last burning

The last witch officially executed in Britain was Janet Horne, burned at Dornoch in 1727. It was an icy day when the poor old woman was dragged from prison – so cold that she held out her hands to warm them before she was thrust into the fire.

An engraving of the hanging of witches, taken from a book on the *Law and Customs of Scotland* by Sir George Mackenzie, 1698.

Scottish witches did not …

- wear steeple hats – they dressed like other people.
- ride on broomsticks – they preferred to sail in eggshells, or fly on bones or pieces of straw.
- often keep black cats – a more usual 'familiar spirit' in Scotland was a hare.
- meet in groups of thirteen – most 'covens' had between two and one hundred witches.

Halloween

Halloween on 31st October is one of Scotland's oldest festivals, pre-dating Christianity by at least a thousand years.

Below: The Scottish tradition of **guising** – or performing a song or verse in return for a penny, or nuts, fruit or sweeties – was not only a Halloween tradition. These guisers from Auchterless in Aberdeenshire are celebrating Hogmanay and the New Year of 1959.

For Celtic people it was **Samhuinn** (Summer's End), and marked the harvest-gathering and winter's beginning. It was also a day for making offerings to ancestral spirits.

When Christianity came, the Church grafted a new festival onto an old one. The first day of November became the **Feast of All Souls** or **Hallowmas**, and the preceding night **All Hallows' Eve** or **Halloween**. The spirits of the dead were believed to visit their old homes, to warm themselves by the fire and take food laid out for them. Fairies, demons and witches were also on the loose.

Superstitious pranks became a feature of this spooky night, with many a game concerned with predicting the future.

Apple magic

Our Celtic ancestors believed that in an undiscovered land there grew a magic apple tree. Legend tells of voyagers crossing the ocean to find the country, called **Emhain Abhlach** (Region of Apples) in Ireland, and in Britain, **Avalon**. At Samhuinn, the apples were safely gathered and the watery custom of **dooking** for apples recalls voyages in search of magic fruit.

Guisers

The bonfire

Although it is now usual to light bonfires on **Guy Fawkes Night** on 5 November, the Halloween bonfire is an older tradition. In the reign of Queen Victoria (1837-1901) the effigy of a witch was burned in front of Balmoral Castle, and all over Scotland people danced around hilltop bonfires. When the fire was out, a creepy ritual sometimes took place. Among the ashes, a stone was laid for each person present. If anyone's stone was missing by the morning, it was an omen of their death before next Halloween.

The traditional choice for a Halloween lantern in Scotland is the turnip or **tumshie**. Nowadays the American idea of using a pumpkin is more popular. It is certainly a lot more easy to carve!

To see the future

- On the stroke of midnight on Halloween, stand in front of a mirror. Take a knife and peel an apple so that the skin comes off in one strip. Throw the skin over your shoulder, and look into the mirror to see the face of your future partner.

- Late at night, eat a salted herring in three bites. Without drinking or speaking, go to bed. In your dreams you will see the one you will marry offering water to quench your thirst.

- Place two nuts on a burning fire. Name one for yourself, the other for the one you love. If you are ill-suited, the nuts will crackle, then one will jump apart. If you are true lovers, they will burn steadily together. The original site of the **Hallowmas Fair** in Edinburgh was the fairy mound now called Calton Hill. On it grew hazel trees, which provided the nuts for this game.

Fun and games

On Halloween, **guisers** painted their faces and put on fancy dress. They went from house to house, carrying turnip lanterns with grotesquely carved faces. In return for singing and reciting, they received apples, nuts and coins. In the Hebrides, Halloween was called **Mischief Night**; ploughs were hidden, gates removed and animals turned loose. This tradition is similar to American **Trick or Treat**, a game unknown in Scotland until recently.

Fairies

Forget frilly frocks, gossamer wings and twinkling wands. Forget fairies dying if children don't clap their hands. Scottish fairies were tougher and far more dangerous than that …

Every country in the world has its own fairy legends. Perhaps Scottish fairies are a folk memory of a small-statured, ancient race who lived here before the Celts. As hunters and herdsmen, they built houses into the hillsides, covering them with turf so that they resembled green mounds. As the more warlike Celts advanced, they withdrew into the hills, becoming secretive and nocturnal.

Imagination wove legends around these people, giving them supernatural powers and turning their underground dwellings into the **fairy knowes** found all over Scotland. Their tiny flint arrows, still seen on moors and hills, became known as **elf-bolts**.

What were fairies like?

Sir Walter Scott wrote around 1800 that the fairies of Scotland were tiny, mischievous and easily offended: 'The usual dress of the Fairies is green … though on the moors they have been sometimes observed in heath-brown. They often ride in invisible procession, when their presence is discovered by the shrill ringing of their bridles.'

In the Hebrides, fairies were seen as fallen angels. In the Lowlands, good fairies – **seely wichts** – were willing to help with household and farmyard work, provided they were treated well. Wicked fairies – **unseely wichts** – enjoyed hurting people, and precautions had to be taken against them.

Elf-bolts

Elf-bolts, also known as **elf-arrows**, were in fact flint arrowheads carved by neolithic man, but found many years later and thought to be the work of other-worldly creatures. These elf-bolts were often worn as a charm to protect the wearer.

Changelings

The worst trick a fairy could play was to snatch a human baby from its cradle, leaving its own instead. Fairy babies, called **changelings**, were hideous and evil-tempered. In Fife, to get rid of a changeling you burned its toes. It then flew howling up the chimney!

A disappearing minister

The Church disapproved of fairy belief, but one minister believed wholeheartedly. A gravestone at Aberfoyle states that the Rev. Robert Kirk died in 1692 – but did he really? After his funeral, Mr Kirk appeared to a friend, claiming that his corpse had been an illusion. In fact, he had been captured by the fairies of nearby Doon Hill. He had, however, one chance of release. On the day of his baby's christening, he said, he would reappear in the church, and his cousin, Grahame of Duchray, must quickly throw a knife over his head. Unfortunately, on the day, poor Duchray was so astonished by the apparition that he dropped the knife. Mr Kirk departed and was never seen again.

In 1691, a strange book called *The Secret Commonwealth of Elves, Faunes and Fairies*, by the Rev. Robert Kirk had been published – causing speculation that the fairies had abducted him because he knew too much!

The fairy flag

At Dunvegan Castle on Skye is the **fairy flag**, given to the MacLeod family by a fairy, who promised help on three occasions when the flag was waved. So far, the flag has been waved twice …

The scene below from William Shakespeare's play *A Midsummer's Night Dream* shows how the 19th-century artist Sir Joseph Noel Paton imagined fairies.

11

Glaistigs and brownies

Among the better type of fairies were **glaistigs** and **brownies**, who were helpful to humans – provided that humans were grateful and kept on their good side!

Of all the weird creatures in Highland folklore, the strangest was the **glaistig**. A skeletal woman in a green dress, she had ankle-length yellow hair and a face resembling 'a grey stone overgrown with lichen'. She liked herding and milking cows, taking only a nightly cup of milk as reward. But she was very touchy, especially if people mocked her appearance, and gave many hard slaps with her bony grey hands.

Brownies were found all over Scotland and northern England. The brownie (see right) was small, ragged and hairy, with a gaping hole instead of a nose. A resident brownie did odd jobs around the farm, usually by night. He never accepted thanks or any payment, and he too was easily offended. Many farmers lost their brownies by treating them disrespectfully.

Tutelary beings

Glaistigs and brownies are called **tutelary beings**, meaning guardians. A less comfortable guardian was the **banshee**, who attached herself to a family and bewailed its misfortunes. In the Highlands, the banshee is sometimes called 'the Little Washer of Sorrow'. She sits ghost-like beside a river, wailing and washing the bloodstained shirt of the next man to die.

The Maiden of Duror

Once there was a glaistig who began life as a human being. Known as 'the Maiden', she was dairymaid on two farms, Glen Duror and Glen-a-Chulish, until one night she was whisked away by the fairies. Eventually she returned as a glaistig, haunting the rocky ravines between the two farms. But she still loved cattle, and was often seen among them.

A grumpy brownie

At Cranshaws in Berwickshire, there once lived a grumpy old brownie, who helped with mowing and threshing corn. All went well until one day the farmer complained in the brownie's hearing that the corn had not been well mowed or stacked neatly in the

New clothes

The surest way to offend your brownie was to be generous, especially if you took pity on his rags and gave him a new suit. This happened at a farm in Glendevon in Perthshire, causing the brownie to stamp off during the night, calling haughtily over his shoulder:

Gie brownie coat, gie brownie sark, [shirt]
Ye'se get nae mair o' brownie's wark!

barn. That night the brownie could be heard stamping in and out of the barn, muttering to himself:

It's no' weel mowed! It's no' weel mowed!
Then it's ne'er be mowed by me again:
I'll scatter it ower the Raven Stane,
And they'll hae some wark e'er it's mowed
again!

By sunrise, the whole harvest had been thrown over nearby Raven Crag into a stream and the brownie had left Cranshaws for ever.

The labour-intensive work of mowing hay is illustrated in this snapshot of farming life at Springhill Farm, at Baillieston, Old Monkland, Lanarkshire, 1935.

Merfolk

Merfolk were at home on land or sea. In every culture, from Ancient Greece and India to Orkney, Shetland and the Hebrides, they were depicted with human head and torso, and a fish's tail.

The **mermaid**, with her comb and looking-glass, was not good news, and sailors feared her. Vain and pitiless, she tempted them to come to her by singing, sometimes to kill them and sometimes to force them down into an underwater world. Sightings were associated with shipwreck and death. Legends of merfolk are found all over Scotland, but especially on northern coasts. It has been suggested that they were really sea cows or dolphins, but witnesses strongly disagree.

its hair … which was long and thick. I had a distinct view of the features, being at no great distance from the rock … on which it was sitting.

William Munro,
Schoolmaster of Reay, Caithness

From a letter to *The Times* newspaper, 8 September 1809

My attention was arrested by the appearance of a figure resembling an unclothed female sitting on a rock extending into the sea, apparently in the action of combing

The last sighting

The last recorded sighting of a mermaid in Scotland was off the Isle of Muck in 1947. An 80-year-old fisherman, known for his truthfulness, claimed to have seen one floating on an abandoned herring box, again combing her hair.

The Blue Men of the Minch

In a dangerous channel between Lewis and the Shiant Islands, lurk the **Blue Men** – evil spirits sometimes called **storm kelpies**. Described as 'blue-coloured … with a long, grey face, and floating from the waist out of the water', these strange creatures lived in caves beneath the sea. They would swim alongside a ship entering the channel, taunting its crew and hoping to wreck it. To make them back off, the captain had to answer them in rhyme:

Blue Man: *We are here, willing and able To haul you down under the waves!*

Captain: *My ship is large and heavy. Do you want it to flatten your caves?*

Mystery mermaid

The can of sardines below is not what it appears to be. Have a closer look!

Explanation on page 40

A rhyme from Fife

*Four and twenty mermaids
Left the port of Leith,
To tempt the fine old hermit
Who lived upon Inchkeith.
No boat, no breeze, no sailing ship,
No craft had they, no oars nor sails;
Their lily hands were oars enough,
Their tillers were their tails.*

Anonymous

Mermaid's tears

On the shore of St Columba's island, Iona, there are pebbles called 'Mermaid's Tears'. In legend, a mermaid fell in love with a saintly monk, who prayed that she would be given human speech, and a human heart and soul. His prayer was answered, but the mermaid was ungrateful, preferring her free, godless underwater life. Whenever she came ashore to meet the monk, she begged to be rid of his gifts. When he refused, she shed tears that petrified at his feet.

Selkies

I am a man upon the land,
I am a selkie in the sea;
And when I'm far frae every
*   strand,*
My dwelling is in Suleskerry.

Traditional rhyme

Stories of **selkies** – also **silkies** and **selchies** – are told in Orkney and Shetland, and also in the Hebrides, Faroe Islands and Scandinavia. Some people believe they are fallen angels; others souls of drowned sailors. Selkies are seals in the ocean, and become human by shedding their sealskin. The skin must be kept carefully, for if it is lost the selkie can never return to the sea. Many tales tell of marriages between selkies and human beings. These usually end in tragedy.

The Great Selkie of Suleskerry

Once a Norwegian girl met a selkie from Orkney. A boy was born to them, then the selkie disappeared. Long afterwards, the woman met on the shore a grey seal who revealed his identity as her child's father,
promised to return, and again vanished beneath the waves. Seven years later, the selkie reappeared, put a gold chain around his son's neck and took him away. Later the lonely mother married a seal-hunter. One day her husband shot an old grey seal and a younger one, around whose neck hung a golden chain. Unaware of his wife's past, he proudly presented it to her. She cried out in horror:

Alas, alas, this woeful fate,
This woeful fate that's been laid on me!
And once or twice she sobbed and sighed:
And her tender heart did brak in three.

MacCodrum of the Seals

In the Hebrides, people believed that seals were servants of the ruler of **Lochlann** (Norway) known as 'The King of Sleep'. The brown-eyed, dark-haired MacCodrum family were allegedly descendants of a North Uist man and a selkie woman, humans by day and seals by night. They were known as **Sliochd nan Ron** – 'People of the Seals'.

The Finfolk

The mysterious **Finfolk** of Orkney lore were, like selkies – amphibious. Wearing skins and paddling kayaks, they were sorcerers whom humans feared and shunned. In winter they lived in the undersea city of Finfolkaheem, returning in summer to the magical Orkney island of Hildaland (renamed in Christian times Eynhallow). The Finfolk legend may have grown from the fear and resentment of visiting fishermen from the north of Norway, who were called **finnar**.

A 17th-century report

Sometime about this country are seen those Men that are called 'Finmen' …

In the year 1684 [one] was seen from Westra, and for a time after they got a few or no fishees: for they have this Remark here, that these 'Finmen' drive away fishes from the place to which they come.

The Rev. James Wallace,
A Description of the Isles of Orkney (1693)

Stranger than fiction …

Sometimes the finnar and their boats were captured, underlining the link between legend and reality. A sealskin-covered kayak was 'catched' in Kirkwall around 1688, and 'the shirt of the barbarous man in the boat', his harpoon, canoe and paddle were sent to the University of Edinburgh.

But not all kayakers came from Scandinavia. Still on display in Marischal Museum, at the University of Aberdeen, is a kayak belonging to 'a hairy man speaking a language no one understood', who was allegedly captured off the Aberdeenshire coast around 1720. Modern research has identified the kayak as belonging to an Inuit from Greenland. He had paddled across the North Atlantic Ocean, resting on ice floes and, perhaps, hitching lifts on whaling ships.

Below: A model of an Inuit kayak from Greenland in the National Museums Scotland. The frame of this type of kayak is made from driftwood, as trees were sparse in the kayak area. The frame would be covered in cured animal skins, either caribou or seal. Kayaks were used for hunting waterfowl, sea-mammals and animals that could be driven into the water, such as caribou.

Kelpies

If you ever see a handsome black horse standing tamely by a river in Scotland, don't venture near!

Horses are intelligent creatures and helpful to humans, unless they are **kelpies**. Then they are very dangerous indeed.

No supernatural creature was ever more feared than the water-horse (Gaelic *each-uisge*) or **kelpie** – so called from the kelp or seaweed entangled in his mane. Usually pictured as an enormous horse with staring eyes and evil temper, the kelpie was a shape-shifter, able to disguise himself in human form. He would then lure his victim to deep water and try to drown him. It was perilous to try to mount a kelpie, for his back was sticky and once up the rider could never dismount again. A wise traveller, however, might suspect a stranger who had dripping seaweed in his hair!

The Kelpie's Stane

One dark, torrential night a man hurrying home arrived at the bridge at Luib to find it swept away in the swollen river Don. Just then, on the other side, he made out a tall stranger who called out and offered to carry him across. In desperation, the traveller accepted. Imagine his horror when, in midstream, his rescuer turned into a fearsome kelpie and began dragging him down to the river bed! There was a terrible struggle before the victim miraculously escaped. As he crawled up the bank, the enraged monster reared up and threw after him a huge boulder, still called the **Kelpie's Stane**.

The kelpie's bridle

There was only one way to tame a kelpie. His shape-shifting power was believed to lie in his bridle and, if a mortal could steal it, he became the kelpie's master. Because a kelpie was as strong as ten ordinary horses, he was much prized, and his bridle could work magic. A bridle, captured from a kelpie near Loch Slochd, was kept in the MacGregor family for many generations.

A kelpie's curse

Once a kelpie, captured by landowner Graham of Morphie, was forced to carry huge stones to build his master's new house. Only when the task was finished was he freed. Just before leaping back into the water, he uttered a curse which was said to have come true:

> *Sair back and sair banes,*
> *Drivin' the Laird o' Morphie's stanes!*
> *The Laird o' Morphie'll never thrive*
> *As lang's the kelpie is alive!*

From *The Journal of a Tour to the Hebrides with Dr Samuel Johnson,* by James Boswell (1785)

There was once a wild beast [in a loch on Raasay], *a sea-horse, which came and devoured a man's daughter. The man lighted a great fire and had a sow roasted on it, the smell of which attracted the monster. In the fire was put a spit. The man lay concealed behind a wall of loose stones … the monster came, and the man with the red hot spit destroyed it.*

In other lands

Water-horses are called:

Nuggle	Orkney
Shoopiltie	Shetland
Cabbyl-Ushtey	Isle of Man
Ceffyl Dwr	Wales
Bäckahästen (Brook Horse)	Sweden
Nykur	Iceland

ISLE OF SKYE from RAASAY

19

Monsters and dragons

The Loch Ness monster – is it fact or fiction?

The evidence is thin, and scientists are scornful. Some photographs are clearly hoaxes. Nonetheless, 'Nessie' remains the best-known monster in the world.

Modern interest in the Loch Ness monster began in 1933 when a London visitor, George Spicer, claimed to have seen it waddling across a lochside road, but rumours go back centuries. Other lochs have similar monsters. Twentieth-century witnesses have described creatures 'giraffe necked' and 'bigger than an elephant' in places as far apart as the

Right: The one-eyed, one-legged, one-handed fachan of Glen Etive, Argyll.

Pentland Firth and the river Clyde. It is hard to discount these sightings altogether.

1400 years ago ...

The first account of the Loch Ness monster was by the Abbot Adomnán of Iona, who told how, in the 6th century, St Columba had put the fear of God into the beast!

'Nessie'

The Loch Ness monster is one of Scotland's most famous tourist attractions. Thousands of visitors flock to the loch, hoping to catch a glimpse of this most elusive of beasts. Many have searched, but few have spotted it!

THE RETURN OF THE LOCH NESS MONSTER!

A tall tale

No doubt the longest sea serpent ever was seen by a man from Kylerhea on Skye, in the strait between the island and the mainland. 'Yes, yes,' he insisted, 'it's the truth I am telling you. One day I saw the fearsome head of the beast going down the Kyle, and it was a week before his tail passed!'

Dragons

In the Lowlands, tales were told of dragons or **worms**, inhabiting caves and terrifying people. In 1802 Sir Walter Scott recorded lines he had read beside a carving of an armed knight attacking a dragon:

> The wode laird of Warriston   [angry]
> Slew the wode worm of Wormistoune …

The knight, Sir John Somerville, killed the dragon by thrusting burning peats down its throat with his lance. In Scott's time the place where the dragon died was known as the Worm's Glen.

The fachan

Not all monsters were serpents. Some were humanoid, which made them even more horrifying. Take the fachan of Glen Etive in Argyll (see opposite page) – ugly enough to induce heart attacks! He had one eye in the middle of his face, one leg and one huge hand sticking out from his chest. It was said of his single tuft of black hair that 'it was easier to take a mountain from the root than to bend that tuft'.

The Devil

The greatest monster in all Scotland was the Devil himself. As Robert Burns wrote in his poem of 1786, 'Address to the Deil':

> O thou, whatever title suit thee,
> Auld Hornie, Satan, Nick or Clootie …

Whatever he might have been called, the Devil was imagined as a huge black figure with horns, red eyes, a tail and cloven hooves, eager to take souls from God and send them to Hell. He was also a master of disguise – up to a point!

The new minister

In Auchtermuchty in Fife, the people were good and went to church on Sundays. This riled the Devil, who dressed up as a minister and came to preach. He did it so well that the congregation begged him to be their new minister! Only one old man, Robin Ruthven, was suspicious. Creeping to the front of the church, he lifted the minister's black gown, saw the cloven hooves beneath and shouted, 'Run for your lives!'

Above: This scene from Robert Burns' famous poem 'Tam o' Shanter' shows a very Scottish version of the Devil (on the right), wearing plaid with a chieftain's feather in his bonnet. It is painted on a tiny snuff-box from the early 19th century.

Stones ot power

We can see why mystery and magic clung to stones, at a time when humans lived close to the earth, feeling vulnerable and small. Enormous standing stones could easily be imagined as giants and monsters by people who felt lonely and afraid.

These charm stones are known as *clachan nathrach* or adder-stones. They were used in the mid-18th century on Lewis in the Outer Hebrides. Tradition says that adders slithered through the holes in the stones to remove or slough off their skins. The stones were used by the islanders to cure diseases in cattle caused, it was believed, by snake-bites.

Before recorded history, some enormous stones were moved and formed into stone circles, where religious rites were performed. It was thought that spirits inhabited some, while others had healing powers. Smaller magic stones were handed down in families, as charms against sickness in humans and cattle – often dipped in water for the invalid to drink.

Christian missionaries accepted the power of stone-belief. Pictish slab stones are often carved with pagan and Christian symbols, and the great stone crosses of the 6th to the 9th centuries display the Sun as well as the Cross.

On a desolate moor in Lewis, known as **Callanish**, stands a prehistoric stone circle, approached by four avenues like the arms of a cross. The Gaelic name is *Fir Chreig*, which means 'False Men'. In legend, the stones were quarrelsome, heathen giants who refused to build a church. When St Kieran visited, they sneered and refused to be baptised. Kieran was furious and turned them all to stone.

Callanish

Holed stones

Holed stones were healing stones. In Brahan wood near Dingwall there is a large holed stone where children were taken to be cured of various illnesses. A fire was lit and the child undressed. Charms were said while first the clothing, then the child, was passed through the hole.

Serpent stones

In the Highlands and the Hebrides, a 'serpent stone' was supposedly formed by snakes entwining themselves and making a hard ball from their spittle and excrement. The snakes tossed the ball into the air, and if it was snatched before it fell, its magic power of healing was assured. But the snatcher had to run, since angry snakes would chase him until stopped by running water!

St Columba's pebbles

The beautiful multi-coloured pebbles from the beach of Iona had been blessed by Columba himself. Sailors carried them as charms against drowning. (See also page 15 for another story about these pebbles.)

A spell for curing cattle
~ 1607 ~

I charge thee for arrow-shot,
For door-shot, for womb-shot,
For eye-shot, for tongue-shot,
For liver-shot, for lung-shot,
For heart-shot all the maist, [most]
To wend out of flesh and bane [pass away]
Into sack and stane;
In the name of the Father, Son
and Haly Ghaist.

Above: The tombs of the Scottish Kings on Iona; and (below) Iona Abbey at sunset.

IONA ABBEY

23

Holy wells and magic waters

*May the Spirit satisfy you
With the water of life.*

Water, the source of life, has always been a powerful force in magic and religion. In medieval times, there were about 600 holy wells in Scotland. Even longer ago, wells, springs and rivers had a guardian spirit, often in the form of a sacred fish. In Christian times, a pagan well simply assumed the name and power of a Christian saint. Holy well water was believed to cure disease; pilgrims came, prayed, drank and sometimes claimed a cure.

The demons' well

St Columba's biographer, Adomnán, tells of a well at Invermoriston, in Inverness-shire, which was possessed by demons. These evil beings ensured that everyone who drank there went home leprous or blind. When Columba arrived and went for a drink, his pagan enemies were delighted, thinking that he too would be stricken by disease. But Columba blessed the well and banished its demons, turning it into a healing well.

Water of baptism

In the north-east of Scotland, the minister baptising a baby had to prevent water from running into its eyes. It was believed that if even a drop of water entered the eyes, it opened them to seeing ghosts. If a boy and a girl were to be baptised at the same ceremony, the parents insisted that the girl went first. A superstition said that if the boy went first, he left his beard in the water – and the girl got it!

ST TRIDUANA'S WELL

It is said that Triduana arrived in Scotland as a young maiden, when making a holy pilgrimage from Rome, or perhaps Hungary, with the relics of St Andrew. She ended up in Restalrig, known as *Lestalryk*, in Lothian, where she devoted her life to prayer and the care of a holy well. This well later became a place of holy pilgrimage for those afflicted with eye-disease.

River magic

Water taken from under a bridge, across which the dead were carried, had special powers, especially if it flowed south. So did water taken from the place where two rivers meet.

A strange cup

At some wells, sick people drank from the horn of a living cow. They believed that the health of the animal might come to them through the water.

St Fillan's Pool

St Fillan's Pool, near Tyndrum, Perthshire, was believed to cure insanity. The patient was led three times round the pool in the name of the Father, Son and Holy Spirit, before being immersed in the icy water. He or she was then taken to nearby St Fillan's Priory, stretched on his back between two sticks and tied up with rope. If he unknotted himself before morning, he would recover. If not, the case was hopeless.

A leper king

Late in life, King Robert the Bruce developed leprosy. He sought a cure at a spring near Ayr, and at Scotlandwell, Kinross. Sadly, the disease killed him.

A clootie well

Near Munlochy, on the Black Isle, is a famous rag well dedicated to St Boniface. Pieces of cloth, or **cloots**, have been attached to surrounding bushes and trees by grateful pilgrims, believing themselves cured after drinking water from the well. The well is an eyesore, but since it is believed that anyone removing a rag will take on the illness of the person who put it there, no one is keen to tidy it up!

This picture of the clootie well located between Tore and Munlochy, Ross-shire, was taken in the 1960s. Clootie wells are associated with healing, sometimes because of the minerals in the water. Some people also believe that, as the cloth rots away, the illness will disappear.

Healing wells and their cures ...

St Triduana's Well in Leith, Edinburgh, and St Ronan's Well at Innerleithen were thought to cure eye-disease, while The Well of Virtues on St Kilda brought relief to those suffering from deafness or nervous diseases. You might help a case of whooping cough or rheumatism by taking the water at St Mary's at Orton, but for skin complaints, try St Katherine's, Liberton, Edinburgh.

Are there any holy wells near where you live? Have a look at the following website:

www.megalithic.co.uk

for information on Cheese Well, near Innerleithen, St Matthew's Well in Roslin, Lady Well in Glasgow, Monks Well at St Andrews, and Holy Well (Chapel of Stoneywood) near Aberdeen.

Beasts great and small

So God created man in his own image … and said, 'Rule over the fish in the sea, the birds of heaven, and every living thing that moves upon the earth'.

These lines from the Book of Genesis, well known to our Bible-reading ancestors, gave humans the task of caring for God's Creation. However badly done, the bond between people and animals has always been intense. We have feared, loved, used, sacrificed and eaten them, given them magical significance and made up stories about them.

Pictish Beasts

Before pen and paper were used in Scotland, Pictish sculptors carved 'symbol stones'. Their meaning is not wholly understood, but animals featured strongly, including snakes, salmon, wolves, stags, bulls and horses. A creature called the 'Pictish Beast' (also 'Dragon' or 'Elephant') appears most often. It may be a figure from a lost Pictish legend.

King of the Cats

One night on his way home, a Borderer met a funeral procession made up entirely of cats! As the coffin, covered with black velvet, passed by, the man was so scared that he legged it all the way home. As he gasped out the story to his wife, a huge black cat entered the kitchen, stood by the fire and waved his tail. 'I am the King of the Cats,' he said, before swiftly vanishing up the chimney!

Bad luck beasts

Fishermen in Fife had many superstitions about animals. They never mentioned pigs, and believed that pork on board a boat would cause a storm. Rabbits were blamed for drowning, but the most unlucky creature was the hare, with its witchy reputation. No one seeing a hare would go to sea that day; even the sight of a dead hare made them tremble.

From *A Description of the Western Isles of Scotland*, by Martin Martin (1695)

The natives [of Skye] have a remark that, when the cows of one person … run up and down the fields, and make a loud noise without any visible cause, that is a presage of the master's or mistress's death. James Macdonald of Capstil, having been killed at the battle of Killiecrankie, it was observed that night that his cows gave blood instead of milk. His family and other neighbours concluded that this was a bad omen.

The fairy dog

The fairy dog (Gaelic: *Cù Sith*) had a dark-green coat. He was kept as a watchdog in fairy hills and was feared by all humans. If he was set loose, he left enormous footprints in earth and snow. When the fairies took him hunting, his baying was so loud that sailors heard it far out at sea.

Mice

Mice were unlucky and believed to bring death to a household. To get rid of them, you pinned the following message on the wall:

> *Ratton and mouse,*
> *Leave the puir woman's house;*
> *Gang awa' owre by to the mill,*
> *And there ane and a' ye'll get your fill.*

With luck, the mice would read it and then depart!

King otter

In Highland tradition, the king otter is unusually large, with only a small white spot on its breast vulnerable to a shot. Because it is so rarely killed, its skin has magic properties. It is said that some of Bonnie Prince Charlie's soldiers at Culloden carried a tiny piece of a king otter's skin. They stayed alive, while those who were unprotected died.

Birds

Happy the craw [crow]
That builds in the Trottenshaw

[poss. in south-east Scotland]

And drinks o' the water o' Dye –
For nae mair may I.

Traditional verse

The lark's song

Up in the lift go we; [sky]
Tee-hee, tee-hee!
There's not a shoemaker on earth
Can make a shoe to me.
Why so? Why so?
Because my heel's as long as my toe!

Anonymous

People have always loved birds, envying their freedom and putting words to their calls.

Many legends feature magic birds, especially swans. In Christian mythology swans are associated with Christ and his saints. In Scotland there are good birds and bad birds, and many rhymes and superstitions about them. The robin (right) was once believed to have a drop of God's blood in its veins. The magpie, however, was cursed because it was the only bird not to wear full black dress at Christ's Crucifixion.

A warning to egg collectors

The laverock and the lintie, [lark; linnet]
The robin and the wren;
If ye harry their nests [raid]
Ye'll never thrive again.

Marriage

There is a tradition that robin and wren are actually husband and wife:

The robin and the wren
Are God's cock and hen.

Swan song

The mute swan is said to sing only once, just before it dies. It is very unlucky to kill a swan. Closeburn Loch in Dumfriesshire is haunted by the ghost of a swan shot there long ago. Pure white with a blood-stained breast, it appears when a member of the Kirkpatrick family is about to die.

The yellowhammer

Long ago, the beautiful yellowhammer was often very badly treated. In Scotland it was called **yellow yorling** or **yellow yite**. The following verse gives a superstitious clue to its unpopularity:

> Hauf a puddock, hauf a toad   [half; frog]
>   Hauf a yellow yorling;
> Drinks a drap o' the deil's bluid   [devil's]
>   Every May morning.

The Great Scree of Culloden

On Culloden Moor there is a ghostly black bird called the 'Great Scree of Culloden'. A sighting means bad luck. It was first seen on 15 April 1746, the eve of the battle, by the Jacobite commander, Lord George Murray. Next day, the Jacobite army suffered a disastrous defeat.

St Kilda legends

The rare visit of a cuckoo to the lonely islands of St Kilda was believed to mean the death of the islands' laird, The MacLeod of MacLeod. The equally rare arrival of a heron was thought to be a visit from a witch of Lewis.

'Flannan Isle'

One stormy night in December 1900, the lighthouse lamp on the remote Flannan Isle (33 kilometres west of Lewis) went out. When the support vessel *Hesperus* called to investigate, the door was locked, the lamp was trimmed, but no fires were lit. Three keepers had vanished and what happened remains a mystery to this day.

Were the men washed away in the storm by a giant wave? In 1912, in his poem 'Flannan Isle', Wilfrid Wilson Gibson (1878-1962) suggested a more sinister fate. Read the poem online at

www.poetry-archive.com/g/ flannan_isle.html

What is the connection between the missing keepers and some very mysterious birds?

Answer on page 40

Above: The steep steps of the east landing place on Flannan Isle, 1898.

Magic plants and trees

The oak, the ash, and the ivy tree,
Flourish best at hame, in the north
countrie. Traditional song

Before modern times, medicine was plant-based and regarded as a branch of magic. Good healers avoided poisonous herbs and used helpful ones to prepare infusions, like modern herbal teas, for both humans and animals. Others were applied externally as poultices and lotions.

Sacred trees

From ancient times, trees played a part in religion and magic. Some were honoured, some feared. The druids, priests and law-givers in Celtic, pre-Christian Scotland revered the oak, with its parasite mistletoe; rowan and hazel were also sacred. Roman observers reported that druids ate acorns and hazelnuts in order to predict the future.

Mistletoe

The magic of mistletoe survived the druids. Near Errol in Perthshire, a huge oak laden with mistletoe was once considered so powerful that the Hays, important local landowners, made it their emblem. They believed that a sprig of mistletoe cut with a new dagger on All Hallows' Eve was a pro-tection against witchcraft, and that a spray put in the cradle prevented the child being stolen by fairies.

The rowan

The rowan, or mountain ash, has always been known as a charm against witchcraft. Often the crossbeam supporting a house roof was made of it. A rowan planted at the door repelled witches, and rowan berries strung on red thread (also magical) might be worn as a good-luck charm. All over Scotland it was said that:

> *Rowan tree and red thread*
> *Make the witches tyne their speed.* [slow]

An unlucky tree

> *Bourtree, bourtree, muckle rung* [bough]
> *Never straight and never strang;*
> *Ever bush and never tree,*
> *Syne Our Lord was nailed to ye!*

There is an old tradition that the elder tree, known as the *bourtree* in Scotland, was used to make the Cross on which Jesus Christ was crucified. Its stunted, crooked appearance was a sign of divine displeasure. In some places it was so unlucky that even to burn it on the hearth was dangerous. Yet its green bark-juice, if applied to the eyelids of a baptised child, was said to give it the power to see fairies.

The yew at Fortingall

In the churchyard at Fortingall, in Glen Lyon near Aberfeldy, there is a famous yew, still living and thought to be about 2000 years old, or even older. Legend holds that Pontius Pilate, who tried and sentenced Christ to death, was born at Fortingall and played under the yew as a child. Because yew is poisonous, it has no healing tradition, but was believed to protect against drowning, danger and confusion.

Hawthorn

There is a persistent belief that to bring hawthorn blossom indoors is worse than unlucky, since its presence dooms a family member to die before the year's end.

THE FORTINGALL YEW

The Fortingall yew is thought to be the oldest living organism in Europe.

Healing herbs

Infusions	good for ...	Lotions and poultices	good for ...
bramble	diarrhoea	ivy	eye infections
nettles	swollen ankles	southernwood	
coltsfoot	coughs and colds	('apple-ringie')	septic wounds
peppermint	indigestion	marigold	corns
camomile	insomnia	seaweed	rheumatism
		leeks	infected fingernails

Saints and miracles

In the New Testament, the word 'saint' simply meant a believer in Jesus Christ.

It is said that St Andrew felt unworthy to be crucified on the same kind of cross as Jesus. The flag of Scotland, called the **Saltire**, shows the type of cross used instead.

Mystery object

Above is part of the treasure hoard found on the site of Candida Casa at Whithorn. With the rings and plate is another object (on the right). Do you know what it is?

Answer on page 40

It was long after the time described in the New Testament that some specially holy people were given the title **'saint'**. Many had suffered and were even killed for their beliefs.

Christianity came to Scotland from two directions, south and west. In the 5th century Ninian, a Christian from Cumbria, built a church at Whithorn in Galloway, which was called **Candida Casa**, the 'Shining White House'. In AD 563, Columba, a princely monk from Ireland, landed on the tiny Hebridean island of Iona with his twelve companions, eager to convert people to faith in Christ. To prove the superiority of their God, the missionaries had to perform miracles which now sound uncomfortably like magic tricks. The new faith triumphed, but old beliefs and superstitions quietly persisted, many into modern times.

St Andrew

Andrew was not a Scot. A fisherman from Galilee, he was one of Jesus's twelve disciples and was eventually crucified. Legend says that around the 10th century St Regulus (or Rule) brought Andrew's bones to Scotland and buried them on the Fife coast. A town called St Andrews formed on the site.

From 'The Prayer of St Columba'

Let me bless almighty God,
whose power extends over sea and land,
whose angels watch over all …
Let me do my daily work,
gathering seaweed, catching fish,
giving food to the poor …
Delightful it is to live
on a peaceful isle, in a quiet cell,
serving the King of kings.

St Kentigern's miracles

Where's the tree that never grew?
Where's the bird that never flew?
Where's the fish that never swam?
Where's the bell that never rang?

Answer to this motto's lines on page 40

St Magnus's boat

Magnus, a descendant of Vikings, was joint ruler of Orkney. A Christian, he was murdered on the order of his pagan cousin in 1116, and later became a saint. In the chapel of Ladykirk on South Ronaldsay, there is a stone with pointed ends, bearing the imprint of human feet. It is said to be St Magnus's boat.

Below is a stained glass window bearing an image of Magnus. The window is in St Magnus Cathedral, founded in 1137, although the window is a 20th-century addition. Why do you think Magnus is depicted bearing a sword?

Answer on page 40

Mountain and hill

*The four great landmarks on the sea
Are Mount-mar, Lochnagar,
        Clochnaben and Bennachie …*

Early rhyme

It is hard to stand anywhere in Scotland and not see, either close by or in the distance, mountain peaks or a range of hills. From the North-West Highlands, south through the Grampians and the Trossachs to the Borders, our high places are among the loneliest, and sometimes spookiest, landscapes in the world.

A phantom army

In the 20th century, two young men were in the Skye mountains studying geology. While camping in a deserted glen at Harta Corrie, they were wakened after midnight by a strange brightness. Opening their tent, they were amazed to see a phantom army of kilted soldiers, fading away in the moonlight. Later they learned that they had camped near the **Bloody Stone**, marker of a cruel battle between MacDonalds and MacLeods three centuries before.

The Urisk

Ben Dorain (Gaelic: *Beinn Dorain*), near Bridge of Orchy in Argyll, is haunted by an **urisk**, a sad, shy monster, half man and half goat. He was banished there by St Fillan.

The Grey Man of Ben Macdui

The lonely Lairig Ghru pass and Ben Macdui (Gaelic: *Beinn MacDuibh*) in the Cairngorms are haunted by a monstrous spectre. Rarely seen as more than a shadow, he is fervently believed in by mountaineers and walkers. Described by one as something 'utterly malign, four-legged and obscenely human, invisible yet solid', his shadowy presence and audible footsteps have caused even the most unimaginative of people to flee the mountain. He has even been heard to speak – unfortunately by someone who didn't know Gaelic!

Fairy hills

Schiehallion, a peak in the Grampians north of Aberfeldy, is *Sìdh Chailleann* in Gaelic, meaning 'Fairy Hill of the Caledonians'. Dumyat, in the Ochils of Clackmannanshire, was also a fairy hill. Legend tells of a miller's wife from the village of Menstrie who was spirited away by fairies. Sad and homesick, she could be heard singing:

Oh, Alva's woods are bonnie,
Tillicoultry's hills are fair,
But the bonnie braes o' Menstrie,
They mak' my hairt aye sair.

The Eildon Hills

The Eildon Hills in the Borders were, said the writer James Hogg, a single peak until they were split in three by a devil. King Arthur and his knights are said to sleep under them. A witch was burned at a spot where grass has never since grown, and it was there that the wizard Thomas the Rhymer met the queen who lured him into Fairyland. It is rumoured that there is a gold mine under the Eildons – suggested by the yellow teeth of the sheep grazing there!

A Lanarkshire hill

On Tintock-tap there is a mist,
And in that mist there is a kist,   [chest]
And in that kist there is a caup,   [cup]
And in that caup there is a drap.
Tak' up the caup
And drink the drap,
And set the caup on Tintock-tap.

Curses and prophecies

Edinburgh castle, toune and tower,
God grant thou sink for sinne,
And that even for the black dinner
Earl Douglas gat therein.

Traditional curse

Nowadays cursing usually means swearing. Historically, it was more sinister. People feared curses, either by witches or enemies. Some curses called for punishment of many for the sin of a few. All Edinburgh was cursed for the betrayal, in 1440, of the young Earl Douglas and his brother, invited to dine at the Castle with the ten-year-old King James II. After a friendly dinner, the guests were murdered by noblemen in front of the horrified king. Prophecies were often like curses, since they predicted ghastly future events. Alarmingly, they had a habit of coming true!

The most famous Highland prophet was Coinneach Odhar (Kenneth MacKenzie), who lived near Dingwall in the 17th century. He is known as the **Brahan Seer**. Using a magic blue stone, he successfully foretold the Battle of Culloden, the cutting of the Caledonian Canal, the coming of railways and of North Sea oil ('A black rain will bring riches to Aberdeen').

A prophesying midwife

At the birth of Archibald Johnston, Lord Warriston, in 1611, the midwife prophesied:

Full moon, high sea,
Great man shalt thou be,
But an ill death shalt thou die.

Fact: After a highly successful career as a lawyer and government servant, Lord Warriston was executed in 1663 by order of King Charles II.

KING CHARLES II

Merlin's grave

In legend, the wizard Merlin was buried at Drumelzier, near the river Tweed. Close by ran a separate stream, the Powsail burn. The 13th-century prophet, Thomas of Ercildoune ('The Rhymer') predicted: *'When Tweed and Powsail meet at Merlin's grave, / Scotland and England shall one monarch have'.*

Fact: On the day in 1603 when the Tweed overflowed and joined the Powsail, Queen Elizabeth of England died. King James VI of Scotland became king of a United Kingdom.

An anonymous warning

*Great Tay of the waves
Shall sweep Perth bare.*

Fact: Although the Tay floods frequently at Perth, this catastrophe hasn't happened … yet.

PERTH, mid-1800s

A prophecy of St Columba

*Iona of my heart, Iona of my love,
Instead of the voices of monks,
shall be lowing of cattle;
But ere the world come to an end,
Iona shall be as it was.*

Fact: The monastery of Iona was destroyed by Vikings in AD 801. It was rebuilt in the 20th century.

The nine of diamonds

In a card game, the nine of diamonds is called 'The Curse of Scotland'. The reference, first printed in 1710, is perhaps to an unpopular Secretary of State, John Dalrymple, Master of Stair (1648-1707), who had ordered the Glencoe Massacre in 1692. There are nine diamonds on the Dalrymple family crest.

The doom of Mar

A 16th-century Earl of Mar took stones from Cambuskenneth Abbey to build a new house in Stirling. The angry Abbot cursed him and his descendants, prophesying that the new house would stand unfinished; the family lands would pass to strangers; a mother would die in a burning house; three children would be born blind; and the curse would end with a kiss of peace when a tree grew on the roof of Alloa Tower.

Fact: Everything that was prophesied actually happened. The 'kiss' was given by Queen Victoria.

JOHN DALRYMPLE

Royal legends

Kings, queens, princes and princesses fascinate ordinary folk. They appear in fairy tales, and even real royals inspire strange legends.

ST MICHAEL'S CHURCH, LINLITHGOW

Were King Arthur and the Round Table knights Scottish, English or Welsh? Place-names like Arthur's Seat or Ben Arthur, Arthur's Stone and Loch Arthur suggest a Scottish connection – but there is no strong evidence that King Arthur ever existed. The Scottish king Macbeth, surrounded in William Shakespeare's play by madness and witches, was actually a good king. But ghosts and marvels do make good stories ….

A Jedburgh ghost

King Alexander III married a French princess, Yolande, at Jedburgh in 1285. The wedding feast was merry until a chilly spectre appeared, tall and thin and wearing grave-clothes. 'Take him and hang him,' shouted the horrified king, but when guards grabbed the intruder, the clothes were empty. It was a grim omen. A few months later the king died, thrown from his horse over a cliff near Kinghorn in Fife. Scotland descended into bloody civil war.

In the words of the earliest known Scots poem:

Qwhen Alexander our king was dede,
That Scotland led in lauche and le,
[law and peace]
Away was sons of ale and brede, [bread]
Of wyne and wax, of gamyne and gle.
[mirth and glee]
Our gold was changit into lede. [led]

The eve of Flodden

The battle of Flodden against the English in 1513 was, as many feared, a total disaster for the Scots. Before the battle, a ghostly old man in a blue gown appeared to King James IV in St Michael's church in Linlithgow, warning him of his death and defeat. Onlookers were appalled, but it was too late. The army moved south next day.

Bonnie Prince Charlie

Many ghosts haunt the fatal battlefield at Culloden, near Inverness. Strangely, the ghost of the Jacobite figurehead Charles Edward Stewart, 'Bonnie Prince Charlie', rarely appears there. The County Hotel in Dumfries (now demolished), where he stayed during his march to and from Derby in England, was haunted by him. In 1936 a guest saw a figure in Jacobite dress, appearing and returning through a closed door. The door, long sealed up, led to the room where Prince Charlie had slept.

An English haunting

The ghost of Mary, Queen of Scots haunts the Talbot Inn at Oundle, Northhamptonshire, where she never stayed. It seems that when Mary's son, King James VI and I, decided to demolish nearby Fotheringay Castle, the innkeeper bought and installed the oak staircase down which the queen had walked to her execution in 1587. On the banister is a tiny crown impressed by her ring. In a room at the top of the stair, visitors hear mysterious footsteps – and a woman's voice wailing.

> In February 1587, at Fotheringay Castle, Mary, Queen of Scots was beheaded for treason at the command of the English queen, her cousin Elizabeth I.

St Fillan's bone

King Robert I (Robert the Bruce) had an arm bone of St Fillan, which he kept in a silver box and carried into battle. Before the Battle of Bannockburn in 1314, a priest secretly removed the bone to a safe place, afraid that the English might steal it. While Robert was praying, however, the empty box opened and shut suddenly. On inspection, the bone was in its usual place. St Fillan, it appeared, was promising the king the victory.

Pilkington Jackson's famous sculpture of King Robert I (Robert the Bruce) was erected in 1964 at the site of the Battle of Bannockburn, near Stirling, where Robert and the Scots Army beat Edward II of England.

39

ANSWERS

Page 15: **Mystery mermaid** – Not only is a mermaid a surprising find in a tin of sardines, but the tin itself is made of soft material made to look like hard metal.

Page 29: **Flannan Isle** – In Wilfred Wilson Gibson's poem, there was no sign of the lighthousekeepers, but three enormous dark birds were briefly seen together on the island. The suggestion is that the keepers had been magically changed into three huge, ugly black birds.

Page 32: **Mystery object** – The object on the right is the top of a crozier or pastoral staff, which would have been carried by a bishop. It looks like a crook and is symbolic of the shepherd who leads his flock, just as the bishop guides his congregation.

Page 33: **St Kentigern's miracles** – The tree that never grew, the bird that never flew, the fish that never swam, the bell that never rang – these are symbols on the coat of arms of the city of Glasgow, whose patron saint is Kentigern (also known as Mungo), who is associated with these miracles.

Page 33: **St Magnus** – The saint is shown bearing a sword because Magnus was a Christian warrior before he became a saint.

ANSWERS – Facts and activities section

Page iii: **Magic places** – (1=C) Loch Ness; (2=D) Culloden battlefield; (3=B) Orkney; (4=A) Shetland; (5=H) Edinburgh; (6=G) Glamis; (7=E) Dunvegan; (8=F) Schiehallon

Page iv: **Word search** – Answers below.

Y	D	R	N	Z	B	M	S	Y	Y	Q	V	Y	U	G
F	R	U	Z	N	K	Y	F	U	L	V	P	T	L	J
D	Y	I	F	U	G	A	B	M	U	L	O	C	A	M
O	U	M	A	R	S	I	S	T	W	C	G	J	G	E
O	G	N	L	F	Z	Z	L	K	Z	H	B	I	N	R
I	S	L	E	G	R	E	T	L	O	P	T	U	I	M
S	N	E	Z	D	E	Q	D	S	A	S	U	X	T	A
G	Y	I	H	I	D	O	T	O	I	H	R	Y	R	I
M	J	R	K	F	M	O	W	A	O	Y	E	Z	O	D
E	A	L	U	M	N	L	L	S	M	K	L	H	H	R
X	E	E	S	E	T	G	N	F	W	U	I	F	C	J
S	F	K	T	R	I	D	U	A	N	A	L	N	X	S
F	L	Y	C	L	N	E	S	S	I	E	R	E	G	D
E	L	L	I	I	J	I	V	H	C	T	I	W	T	C
C	B	C	R	N	R	O	W	A	N	A	L	T	V	S

ANSWERS
Facts and activities section (*cont'd*)

Page v: **Criss-crossword** – (1) Fachan; (2) Glaistig; (3) Scourie; (4) Hare; (5) Horse; (6) Selkies; (7) Iona; (8) Nykur; (9) King Otter

Page vi: **Who am I?** – (A) St Columba; (B) Coinneach Odhar, the Brahan Seer; (C) Mary, Queen of Scots; (D) Thomas de Quincey; (E) Rev. Robert Kirk; (F) Robert the Bruce; (G) James VI and I; (H) Sir Walter Scott; (I) Bonnie Prince Charlie

USEFUL WEBSITES

BBC www.bbc.co.uk/scotland/history/

Fife – folklore and history
www.fife.50megs.com/scots-folklore-fairies.htm
www.fife.50megs.com/scots-folklore-fishermens-superstitions.htm
www.fife.50megs.com/scots-folklore-magic-wells.htm

Glasgow – folklore and history
www.scotland-guide.co.uk

Isle of Iona – for the history of Iona abbey
www.isle-of-iona.com/abbey.htm

National Museums Scotland
www.nms.ac.uk

National Trust for Scotland – for the history of the Battle of Culloden
www.nts.org.uk/culloden

Orkneyjar – for accounts of merfolk and selkies, and general introduction to the islands
www.orkneyjar.com

Scottish history
www.undiscoveredscotland.co.uk

University of Aberdeen – for information about Marischal Museum
www.abdn.ac.uk/marischal_museum/

Wikipedia
www.wikipedia.org

Witches and witchcraft
www.shc.ed.ac.uk/Research/witches

Supernatural Scotland
Facts and activities

from 'Tam o' Shanter'

This book belongs to:

_____

Write your name on the above line.

Read Robert Burns' poem about 'Tam o' Shanter' and his encounter with the ghostly beings that haunted Auld Alloway Kirk near the town of Ayr.

Scottish weather

Before scientific forecasting, Scots
folk had far more traditional ways
of anticipating the weather!

When craws gang crowin' tae their beds,
They'll rise in the morn wi' watery heads.

*

If the evening's red, and the morning grey,
It is the sign o' a bonnie day;
If the evening's grey and the morning's red,
The lamb and the ewe will go wet to bed.

*

When Falkland Hill puts on his cap,
The Howe o' Fife will get a drap.

*

If the oak afore the ash,
Then we're gaun tae hae a splash:
If the ash afore the oak,
Then we're gaun tae hae a soak.

*

Wild geese, wild geese, ganging tae the sea,
Good weather it will be.
Wild geese, wild geese, ganging to the hill,
The weather it will spill.

*

Aboot the moon is there a brugh?   [halo]
The weather will be cauld and rough.

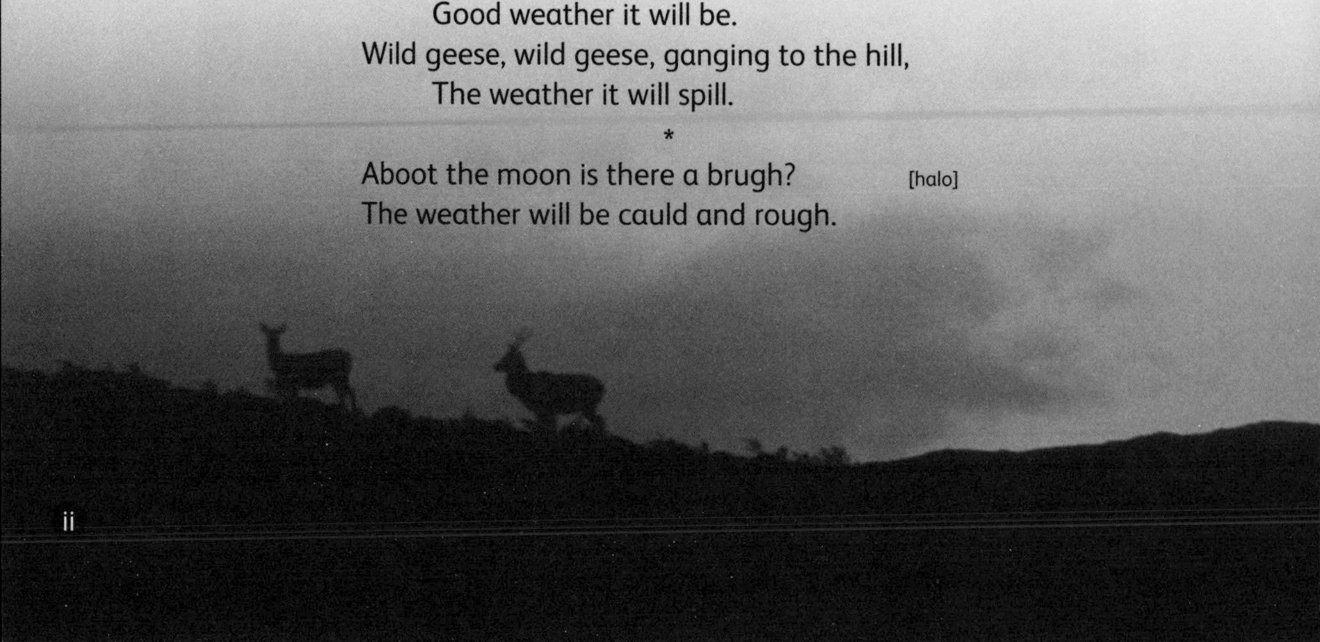

Magic places

Using a map of Scotland with place names, try to match the letter to the number at these supernatural spots:

(**1**) = monster's loch (see p. 20)

(**2**) = haunted battlefield (p. 3)

(**3**) = selkie islands (p. 16)

(**4**) = home of the shoopiltie (p. 19)

(**5**) = a ghostly capital (p. 2)

(**6**) = most haunted castle (p. 5)

(**7**) = home of fairy flag (p. 11)

(**8**) = fairy hill (p. 35)

Answers on page 40

Word search

Move diagonally, as well as up and down, in any direction, to discover the 18 words listed below that are associated with supernatural Scotland.

Answers on page 40

Y	D	R	N	Z	B	M	S	Y	Y	Q	V	Y	L	G
F	R	U	Z	N	K	Y	F	U	L	V	P	T	L	J
D	Y	I	F	U	O	A	B	M	U	L	O	C	A	M
O	U	M	A	R	S	I	S	T	W	C	G	J	G	E
O	G	N	L	F	Z	Z	L	K	Z	H	B	I	N	R
T	S	I	E	G	R	E	T	L	O	P	T	U	I	M
S	N	E	Z	D	E	Q	D	S	A	S	U	X	T	A
G	Y	I	H	I	D	O	T	O	I	H	R	Y	R	I
M	J	P	K	F	M	O	W	A	O	Y	E	Z	O	D
E	A	L	U	M	N	L	L	S	M	K	L	H	F	R
X	E	E	S	E	T	G	N	F	W	U	I	F	C	J
S	F	K	T	R	I	D	U	A	N	A	L	N	X	S
F	L	Y	C	L	N	E	S	S	I	E	R	E	G	D
E	L	L	I	I	J	I	V	H	C	T	I	W	T	C
C	B	C	P	N	R	O	W	A	N	A	L	T	V	S

AMULET	FORTINGALL	MERMAID	SELKIE
COLUMBA	GHOST	NESSIE	TRIDUANA
DOOKING	GLAISTIG	PICTS	YORLING
FAIRY	KELPIE	POLTERGEIST	
FLODDEN	MERLIN	ROWAN	

Criss-crossword

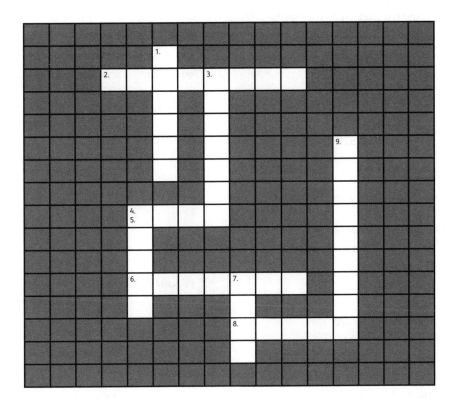

Answer the following questions to complete this word puzzle.

1. Which creature had a single eye and a single arm? (See pages 20-21)

2. Which creature had a face 'like a grey stone overgrown by lichen? (See page 12)

3. Where did Morag the Storm Witch live? (See page 7)

4. (across) What was the name of the murderer William Burke's accomplice? (See page 2)

5. (down) Which animal haunts Haddington House? (See page 4)

6. What name is given to the seal people of the Northern Isles? (See page 16)

7. Where would you find St Columba's pebbles? (See page 23)

8. What is a water-horse called in Iceland? (See page 19)

9. Which mammal is vulnerable to a shot only on a white spot on its breast? (See page 27)

Answers on page 40

Who am I?

All the following were real people and are mentioned in this book. Can you work out who they are from the clues? Write their names on the last line.

Answers on page 40

A

Born:	*circa* AD 521
at:	Gartan, Ireland
educated:	Moville and Leinster, Ireland
lived in:	Derry; Durrow; and Isle of Iona
occupation:	abbot and author
died:	597, of old age, at Iona

I AM: ....

B

Born:	around 1520
at:	Uig, Isle of Lewis
educated:	Isle of Lewis
lived in:	Isle of Lewis, Easter Ross
occupation:	prophet
died:	1577, burned alive, at Brahan Castle, Easter Ross

I AM: ....

C

Born:	1542
at:	Linlithgow
educated:	France
lived in:	St Germain, France; Edinburgh; Northamptonshire in England
occupation:	ruler of a country
died:	1587, beheaded at Fotheringay, in England

I AM: ....

D

Born:	1785
at:	Manchester, England
educated:	Bath and Oxford University, England
lived in:	London; The Lake District, England; Lasswade
occupation:	author
died:	1859, of opium addiction, in Edinburgh

I AM: ....

E

Born:	1644
at:	Aberfoyle
educated:	High School of Dundee; universities of Edinburgh and St Andrews
lived in:	Balquhidder, Aberfoyle
occupation:	minister, author and fairy expert
died:	disappeared in 1692, at Aberfoyle

I AM: ....

F Born: 1274

at: Turnberry

educated: as a warrior

lived in: Ayrshire; Scone; Stirling; and Rathlin, Ireland

occupation: king and hero

died: 1329, of leprosy, at Cardross on the Firth of Clyde

I AM: ………………………………

H Born: 1771

at: Edinburgh

educated: Royal High School, Edinburgh; Moffat Academy; Edinburgh University

lived in: Edinburgh; Scottish Borders

occupation: lawyer and author

died: 1832, of a stroke, at Abbotsford, near Melrose

I AM: ………………………………

G Born: 1566

at: Edinburgh

educated: by tutor, George Buchanan

lived in: Edinburgh and London

occupation: ruler of a country, scholar and witch-hunter

died: 1625, of dysentery, at Theobalds in Hertfordshire

I AM: ………………………………

I Born: 1720

at: Rome, Italy

educated: France

lived in: Italy; France; Scottish Highlands

occupation: prince and claimant to a throne

died: 1788, of a stroke, in Rome

I AM: ………………………………

PLACES OF INTEREST

Listed below are a number of places associated with the histories and mysteries of supernatural Scotland!

Visitor Centres

Inverness-shire
Culloden Centre, near Inverness
Loch Ness Exhibition Centre, Drumnadrochit
Stirling
  Bannockburn Heritage Centre, Whins of Milton
Western Isles
Iona Heritage Centre, Isle of Iona
Callanish Standing Stones and Visitor Centre, Isle of Lewis

Castles, churches, houses, museums

Aberdeenshire
  Museum of Scottish Lighthouses, Fraserburgh; **Marischal Museum**, University of Aberdeen

Ayrshire
  Alloa Tower, Alloa
  Alloway Auld Kirk, Alloway
  Robert Burns Museum, Alloway
Clackmannanshire
Edinburgh
  Edinburgh Castle
  National Museum of Edinburgh
  Palace of Holyroodhouse
  St Triduana's Chapel, Restalrig Church
Glasgow
  St Mungo's Museum of Religion and Art
Inverness-shire
  Groam House Museum, Rosemarkie
  Highland Folk Museum, Kingussie
  Urquhart Castle, Loch Ness
Orkney Islands
  Orkney Faerie Museum and Gallery, Westray
Perthshire – Meigle Sculpture Museum, Meigle
Scottish Borders
  Abbotsford House, by Galashiels
West Lothian
  St Michael's Parish Church, Linlithgow

FURTHER CREDITS

CASSELL'S *OLD AND NEW EDINBURGH: Its History, its People, and its Places* by James Grant (Cassell & Co: London, n.d.) – for activities section vi (Bonnie Prince Charlie)

THE COMPREHENSIVE HISTORY OF ENGLAND: Civil, Military, Religious, Intellectual and Social by Charles Macfarlane and Rev. Thomas Thomson (Blackie & Son: Glasgow, Edinburgh & London) (no date) – for pp 37 (Perth); Activities section vii (Mary, Queen of Scots)

LITERARY LANDMARKS OF EDINBURGH by Laurence Hutton (Osgood, McIlvaine & Co: London, 1891) – for pp 5 and activities section vii (Thomas de Quincey and cottage)

POPULAR TALES OF THE WEST HIGHLANDS by John F. Campbell (Edmonston and Douglas: Edinburgh, 1862) – for p. 20 (the fachan)

SCOTTISH PICTURES drawn with pen and pencil by Samuel G Green (Religious Tract Society: London, 1891) – for pp 19 (Raasay, Skye); 23 (Tombs of the Scottish Kings, Iona);

© DUNCAN ANDERSON – for page 35 (Eidon Hills)

© MARTIN AND DANIEL AULD – for pp 9 (apples and pumpkin lantern); 16 (seal); 28 (robin, swan); 29 (heron)

© SHEILA CANT – for pp 12 (brownie); 13 (Maiden of Duror); 14 (mermaid); 16 (selkies); 18 (kelpie); 19 (kelpie); 26 (Pictish stone); 27 (mice and rabbits); 30 (ivy)

HISTORIC SCOTLAND (© Crown copyright reproduced courtesy of Historic Scotland www.historicscotlandimages.gov.uk) – for pp 33 (St Magnus stained glass window); 38 (St Michael's Church, Linlithgow)

NATIONAL GALLERIES OF SCOTLAND – for pp 11 (© Sir Joseph Noel Paton/*The Reconciliation of Oberon and Titania* 1847/ National Gallery of Scotland [detail]); 39 (Unknown Artist/ *Execution of Mary, Queen of Scots*/Scottish National Portrait Gallery

NATIONAL TRUST FOR SCOTLAND (© Reproduced by kind permission of The National Trust for Scotland Photo Library) – for page 34 (Glencoe); 37 (*John Dalrymple*/photo: John Sinclair)

© PAUL TURNER – for pages 4 (ruins in graveyard); 18 (waterfall); 23 (Iona Abbey); 24 (St Triduana's Well); 31 (Fortingall churchyard and yew); Activities section, page ii (stags on hillside)

© JOHN DOUGLAS WILSON – for Activities section, page vii (Scott Monument)

OTHER TITLES IN THE NEW SCOTTIES SERIES (eds Frances and Gordon Jarvie)

The Clans (Gordon Jarvie)
Flight in Scotland (Frances and Gordon Jarvie)
Greyfriars Bobby: A Tale of Victorian Edinburgh (Frances and Gordon Jarvie)
The Jacobites (Antony Kamm)
Mary, Queen of Scots (Elizabeth Douglas)
Robert Burns in Time and Place (Frances and Gordon Jarvie)
Scotland's Vikings (Frances and Gordon Jarvie)
Scottish Rocks and Fossils (Alan and Moira McKirdy)
Scottish Kings and Queens (Elizabeth Douglas)